FLAVORS FROM THE GRILL

CONTENTS

THE BEST RECIPES FOR THE GRILL

There's a long tradition of roasting over an open fire, and this simple, time-tested cooking technique has inspired many excellent meat, fish, and vegetable dishes. From the grills of these six regions come classic dishes as well as new favorites.

NORTH AMERICA & AUSTRALASIA

The barbecue is very popular in the United States, Australia and New Zealand, where it's an occasion for outdoor get-togethers. At these festive events, family and friends enjoy all kinds of grilled delicacies. Juicy steaks, zesty spareribs, baked potatoes, and corn on the cob are always crowd-pleasers. Sauces and marinades—spicy, mild, or sweet—lend vibrant flavor to the hearty fare.

ASIA & THE FAR EAST

Succulent grilled chicken, beef, and vegetable dishes are specialties of Asian cuisine. Skewered meats—marinated or cooked tandoori-style—are particular favorites.

NORTHERN & EASTERN EUROPE

On warm, breezy summer nights, the gardens of Northern and Eastern Europe fill with the tempting aromas of grilled meat and vegetables. These feasts often begin at dusk and continue until the wee hours, as people linger and take

THE MEDITERRANEAN

In this sun-drenched region, outdoor cooking and eating are simple joys of daily life. Best-loved dishes from the grill include marinated seafood, tender meat, and vegetables drizzled with tangy vinaigrette.

LATIN AMERICA & THE CARIBBEAN

Spicy ingredients and condiments are always found by the grill in Latin America and the Caribbean. Colorful chiles, chunky salsas, and flavor-packed sauces give flame-cooked dishes their piquant flair. Locally harvested corn on the cob cooks over coals alongside such entrées as lime-marinated steak, and fish that's fresh from the sea. Lively music often accompanies the fragrant, sizzling food.

advantage of the pleasures of the season. Robust sausages and herb-laced potato salads accompany thick steaks and delicate fish that are cooked to perfection over glowing coals. Beer and wine are always on hand for refreshment.

THE MIDDLE EAST

In the busy marketplaces of this region, street vendors selling skewered meat and chicken provide busy shoppers with quick, economical nourishment. Yogurt, chickpeas, and sauces complement the savory morsels.

PEPPER STEAK AND HERBED TOMATOES

USA

In this American classic, thick steaks are rubbed with fresh black pepper and steeped in a flavor-packed marinade, then grilled alongside juicy, foil-wrapped tomatoes.

INGREDIENTS
(Serves 4)

- 1 large onion
- ⅓ cup vegetable oil
- ¼ cup brandy or orange juice
- 2 tablespoons ketchup
- 1 tablespoon Worcestershire sauce
- 1 tablespoon prepared mustard
- ¼ teaspoon hot sauce
- 2 tablespoons black peppercorns
- 4 shell or strip steaks (about 10 ounces *each*)

FOR THE TOMATOES
- 2 tablespoons olive oil
- 4 tomatoes
- 2 tablespoons chopped fresh parsley
- salt and pepper

1 Peel and finely chop the onion and place in a large bowl. Stir in the vegetable oil, brandy, ketchup, Worcestershire sauce, mustard, and hot sauce. Place the steaks in a large glass baking dish.

2 Coarsely crush the peppercorns in a mortar or blender; pat all over the steaks. Pour the marinade over the steaks, turning to coat. Let rest for 1 hour. Prepare the grill.

3 Brush four pieces of aluminum foil with the olive oil. Cut a ½-inch-deep cross into the top of each tomato. Sprinkle with the parsley and salt and pepper. Wrap each tomato in the prepared foil. Place the tomatoes on the grill; cook for 15 minutes.

4 Meanwhile, remove the steaks from the marinade and sprinkle with salt. Place on the grill and cook for about 10 minutes, turning once, for medium-rare. Let the steaks rest for 5 minutes, then place a steak and a tomato on each of 4 individual plates.

Step 1

Step 3

Step 4

Preparation: 15 minutes
Marinating: 1 hour
Grilling: 15 minutes
Per serving: 764 cal; 51 g pro; 55 g fat; 11 g carb.

TYPICALLY AMERICAN
Since the days of the Spanish cowboys, the barbecue (from the Spanish *barbacoa*) has been an important cultural institution of the American Southwest. More than just a meal, the barbecue is used to celebrate everything from housewarmings to political campaigns.

COOKING TIP

Before serving, let the steaks sit for a few minutes on aluminum foil. That way, the meat will stay juicy. During cooking, the juice tends to concentrate in the center of the steak and needs a couple of minutes to distribute itself throughout the meat again.

SERVING TIPS

Offer your favorite steak sauce with the entree, and serve with baked potatoes and a mixed salad.

Serve a hearty red wine, such as a Cabernet Sauvignon or a Merlot.

ℬARBECUED SPARERIBS

USA

In a typical barbecue meal, you get sizzling, juicy pork ribs smothered in a sweet-sour sauce. Napkins are essential, though many prefer to lick their sticky fingers clean.

INGREDIENTS

(Serves 6)

- 5 pounds pork spareribs
- 1 tablespoon chili powder
- salt and pepper

FOR THE BARBECUE SAUCE

- 1 onion
- 2 garlic cloves
- 1 tablespoon vegetable oil
- ½ cup ketchup
- ¼ cup cider vinegar
- 3 tablespoons Worcestershire sauce
- 3 tablespoons brown sugar
- 2 tablespoons lemon juice
- 2 tablespoons prepared mustard

INGREDIENT TIP

You can substitute baby back or country-style pork ribs for the spareribs.

1 Cut the pork slab into individual ribs, then sprinkle with the chili powder and ½ tablespoon *each* salt and pepper. Let the pork rest for 1 hour, or cover and refrigerate overnight.

2 Preheat the oven to 400°F. Peel the onion and garlic and finely chop. Place the oil in a medium saucepan over medium heat. Add the onion and garlic and cook, stirring occasionally, until softened, about 6 minutes. Stir in the ketchup, cider vinegar, Worcestershire sauce, brown sugar, lemon juice, mustard, and ½ cup water.

3 Bring to a simmer, then cook gently, partially covered, until thickened, about 10 minutes. Remove from the heat. Place the ribs in a single layer in a roasting pan or on a heavy baking sheet. Place in the oven and roast for 1 hour or until the ribs are tender.

4 Prepare a grill. Brush the ribs with the barbecue sauce and grill until nicely browned, turning and brushing with more sauce as necessary, about 10 minutes.

Step 1

Step 3

Step 4

Preparation: 10 minutes
Marinating: 1 hour
Grilling: 1 hour 15 minutes
Per serving: 684 cal; 45 g pro; 47 g fat; 19 g carb.

TYPICALLY CALIFORNIAN

Nowhere else in America does one encounter the aroma of grilled delicacies more than in the state of California. Barbecues here include all the classic ingredients—meat, vegetables, and bread—grilled over an open fire.

COOKING TIP

For a spicy-sweet sauce, mix together ¼ cup *each* oil, soy sauce, and honey, 2 tablespoons *each* Worcestershire sauce and steak sauce, and 1 tablespoon tomato paste. Brush the glaze on the ribs, then roast and grill or broil.

SERVING TIPS

Serve any leftover sauce with the ribs. A crisp salad and corn on the cob rounds out the meal.

 Iced tea, or California red wine from the Napa Valley, makes a harmonious accompaniment.

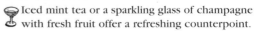 **SERVING TIPS** Fresh green salad and sliced juicy tomatoes go well with these side dishes.

Iced mint tea or a sparkling glass of champagne with fresh fruit offer a refreshing counterpoint.

SCRUMPTIOUS SIDE DISHES

USA

Here's a trio of recipes for the fixin's that typically supplement an American BBQ—steaming potatoes, fresh corn, and garlic bread. Put them on the fire in the order of their cooking times.

INGREDIENTS
(Serves 4)

FOR THE BAKED POTATOES
- 4 large baking potatoes
- seasoned salt

FOR THE CORN ON THE COB
- 4 ears of fresh corn
- 2 tablespoons butter, melted
- 2 tablespoons chopped fresh parsley
- salt and black pepper
- a pinch of cayenne pepper

FOR THE GARLIC BREAD
- 1 large baguette
- 1½ teaspoons olive oil
- 4 garlic cloves
- ½ stick (4 tablespoons) butter, softened
- 2 tablespoons minced mixed fresh herbs
- salt and black pepper

1 Prepare the grill. Scrub and rinse the potatoes; poke several times with a fork. Place each potato on a sheet of aluminum foil; sprinkle with seasoned salt. Wrap up and seal the foil around the potatoes.

2 Shuck the corn and remove the silks. Rinse and dry. Place each ear on a sheet of aluminum foil. In a small bowl, mix the butter, parsley, ¼ teaspoon *each* salt and black pepper, and the cayenne. Brush the mixture over the corn. Wrap up and seal the foil around the corn.

3 Without cutting all the way through, slice the baguette at an angle into 1½-inch slices. Brush a sheet of foil with the olive oil. Pass the garlic through a garlic press.

4 In a small bowl, mix the garlic, butter, herbs, and ¼ teaspoon *each* salt and pepper. Using a knife, spread the garlic butter in between the slices of bread. Wrap up and seal the foil around the bread.

5 Cover and grill the potatoes for about 50 minutes, the corn for 20–30 minutes, and the baguette for about 15 minutes, turning everything occasionally.

Step 1

Step 2

Step 4

Preparation: 40 minutes
Grilling: 15–50 minutes
Per serving: 773 cal; 19 g pro; 24 g fat, 126 g carb.

TYPICALLY AMERICAN
The quintessential American barbecue always features plenty of hearty food. When grilling, toppings and side dishes—such as potatoes, salads, steak sauces, and ketchup—are just as important as the main fare.

$\mathscr{F}$ETA-STUFFED CHICKEN BREASTS

AUSTRALIA

Juicy chicken breasts filled with hearty, piquant feta cheese are served on a colorful bed of fresh vegetables. The dish offers an enticing contrast of tender and crisp, creamy and crunchy.

INGREDIENTS
(Serves 6)

FOR THE SALAD
- ⅓ cup lemon juice
- ¼ cup olive oil
- ¼ cup white wine vinegar
- salt and pepper
- 1 bunch of radishes
- 4 small tomatoes
- ½ cucumber
- 2 small bell peppers (1 green, 1 red)
- 1 cup thawed frozen corn
- 1 ripe avocado

FOR THE CHICKEN
- 8 ounces feta cheese
- 1 large egg
- 2 tablespoons chopped fresh parsley
- 6 chicken breast halves (about 4 ounces each)
- 1½ tablespoons olive oil
- hot or sweet paprika

1 In a large bowl, whisk together the lemon juice, olive oil, vinegar, ¾ teaspoon salt, and ¼ teaspoon pepper. Thinly slice the radishes. Cut each tomato into 8 wedges. Peel and slice the cucumber. Cut the peppers into thin strips. Drain the corn. Add these vegetables to the bowl with the dressing and toss well. Set aside.

2 Prepare the grill. Crumble the feta. In a bowl, stir in the feta with the egg, parsley, and a pinch *each* of salt and pepper. Rinse the chicken breasts and pat dry. Cut a horizontal slit to make a pocket in each. Fill with the feta and secure with toothpicks to enclose the filling. Brush with the oil, then sprinkle with salt, pepper, and paprika.

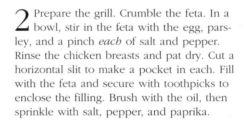

Step 2

Step 2

3 Cook the chicken on the hot grill until nicely browned and opaque throughout, about 10 minutes, turning once. Let stand for 5 minutes. Meanwhile, peel and pit the avocado, then thinly slice.

Step 4

4 Divide the salad among 6 plates and arrange the avocado slices on each. Remove the toothpicks from the chicken, then slice and place on the portions of salad.

Preparation: 40 minutes
Grilling: 15 minutes
Per serving: 452 cal; 35 g pro; 28 g fat; 16 g carb.

TYPICALLY AUSTRALIAN
The cooking traditions of the Aborigines, the indigenous inhabitants of Australia, merged with those of the European settlers to form an interesting hybrid cuisine.

COOKING TIP

For variation, season and grill unfilled chicken breasts until crisp and serve them with a fresh mango sauce: Puree the flesh of 1 ripe mango with the juice of 1 orange, a pinch of chili powder, and 1 tablespoon Asian sweet-and-sour sauce in a blender. Add salt and hot sauce to taste.

SERVING TIPS

Garlic or herb-buttered bread goes irresistibly well with this succulent chicken dish.

Serve a glass of chilled Chablis, draft beer, or mineral water with lemon wedges.

GARLICKY LAMB CHOPS

NEW ZEALAND

INGREDIENTS
(Serves 6)

- 12 (5-ounce) lamb chops
- 8 large garlic cloves
- salt and pepper
- ¼ cup olive oil
- 3 tablespoons lemon juice
- 1 teaspoon dried thyme
- 1 teaspoon dried oregano
- 4 tomatoes
- 8 ounces fresh mozzarella
- fresh basil leaves

INGREDIENT TIP

New Zealand exports not only excellent lamb but also first-rate farm-raised venison. Beef and venison steaks are equally suitable alternates for this recipe.

This recipe combines tender lamb, a New Zealand favorite, with a fresh tomato-mozzarella salad for an ensemble that's sure to please fans of the grill.

1 With a sharp knife, cut a horizontal pocket in the curved side of each lamb chop. Pat the chops dry with paper towels.

2 Peel the garlic and pass through a garlic press. Place the garlic paste into a small bowl and add ¼ teaspoon pepper, 2 tablespoons of the oil, the lemon juice, thyme, and oregano. Spread some of the mixture in the pocket of each chop and rub the remainder over the chops. Place the chops on a plate, cover with foil, and refrigerate for 1 hour.

3 Prepare the grill. Thinly slice the tomatoes and mozzarella and arrange them in alternating slices on 4 plates. Between each slice of mozzarella and tomato place a basil leaf. Sprinkle lightly with salt and pepper and drizzle with the remaining 2 tablespoons olive oil.

4 Place the chops onto the hot grill and grill for 3–5 minutes, turning them with tongs several times. Arrange the chops next to the tomato mozzarella slices.

Step 1

Step 2

Step 3

Preparation: 30 minutes
Marinating: 1 hour
Grilling: 5 minutes
Per serving: 689 cal; 45 g pro;
52 g fat; 8 g carb.

TYPICALLY NEW ZEALAND
Lambs are the prized livestock of many New Zealand farmers; the tender, high-quality meat is exported around the world. "Hogget"—spit-roasted lamb yearling—is a classic New Zealand dish.

COOKING TIP

Keep an eye on the meat as it grills. Depending on
the heat of the coals and the position of the chops,
the meat can quickly overcook. Use tongs instead of a
fork to turn the chops so you won't lose any flavorful
juices to the fire.

SERVING TIPS

Cut out puff pastry dough with
small cutters, brush with butter,
and bake. Serve with the chops.

 For a refreshing match, try an ice-cold
beer or an apple spritzer with lemon slices.

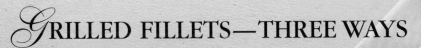

GRILLED FILLETS—THREE WAYS

Juicy grilled cuts of meat are loved throughout the world.
Here are three examples of how varied these dishes can be.

FILET MIGNON CHURRASCO

Preparation: 20 minutes   Marinating: 12 hours   Grilling: 6 minutes

BRAZIL

(SERVES 4)
- 2 small red onions
- 4 garlic cloves
- salt and black pepper
- 2 bay leaves
- ½ cup olive oil
- ¼ cup lime juice
- ¼ cup red wine
- 4 filets mignons (6 ounces *each*), ½-inch thick
- 1 serrano chile
- 3 tablespoons chopped fresh cilantro

1 Peel 1 onion and 2 garlic cloves. Finely chop the onion and place in a glass baking dish.

Pass the peeled garlic through a press. Crush the bay leaves. Add the garlic, bay leaves, half of the oil and lime juice, and the wine to the onion. Add the steaks; turn to coat. Cover; refrigerate for 12 hours.

2 Prepare the grill. For the sauce, peel and chop the remaining onion and garlic; place in a small bowl. Seed and mince the chile. Add the chile, remaining oil and lime juice, and the cilantro to the sauce.

3 Season the steaks with ¼ teaspoon *each* salt and black pepper. Grill for 6 minutes, turning once. Serve the steaks with the sauce.

GRILLED SIRLOIN &

Preparation: 20 minutes

GERMANY

(SERVES 4)
- 1 stick (4 ounces) butter, softened
- 1 tablespoon Dijon mustard
- 1 tablespoon lemon juice
- salt and pepper
- 4 shell or strip steaks (6 ounces *each*)
- 8 bacon strips

1 Prepare the grill. In a small bowl, mix the butter with the mustard, lemon juice, ¼ teaspoon salt, and a pinch of pepper. Place in a pastry

MUSTARD BUTTER

Grilling: 10 minutes

bag fitted with a star tip and pipe out onto a plate in rose shaped dollops. Refrigerate.

2 Season the steaks with ¼ teaspoon *each* salt and pepper and grill for 10 minutes, turning once. Meanwhile, place the bacon on a sheet of foil and place it on the grill. Cook until crisp, turning often.

3 Arrange the steaks and bacon on individual serving plates. Place 1 rosette of the mustard butter next to each steak. Pass the remaining butter rosettes on the side.

SWEET-AND-SOUR PORK FILLETS

Preparation: 40 minutes   Marinating: 1 hour   Grilling: 8 minutes

CHINA

(SERVES 4)
- ½-inch piece fresh ginger
- 5 tablespoons oil
- 3 tablespoons sherry
- 2 tablespoons soy sauce
- pepper
- 8 thick slices of pork tenderloin (1½ pounds)

FOR THE BARBECUE SAUCE
- 2 garlic cloves, peeled
- ⅓ cup chicken broth
- 3 tablespoons white vinegar
- 2 tablespoons sherry
- 1 tablespoon soy sauce
- 3 tablespoons brown sugar
- 2 teaspoons cornstarch
- 2 tablespoons oil
- 1 small leek, the white portion only, minced

1 Peel and mince the ginger; place in a glass baking dish. Add 5 tablespoons oil, 3 tablespoons sherry, 2 tablespoons soy sauce, and ¼ teaspoon pepper. Add the pork; turn to coat. Cover; refrigerate 1 hour.

2 Prepare the grill. Chop the garlic. In a cup, mix the broth, vinegar, sherry, soy sauce, sugar, and cornstarch.

3 Heat 2 tablespoons oil in a wok; sauté the garlic and leek for 1 minute. Add the broth mixture. Boil for 1 minute, stirring. Keep warm.

4 Grill the pork for 6–8 minutes, turning it once. Serve with the barbecue sauce.

17

ᏚWORDFISH WITH SPICY SALSA

THE CARIBBEAN

A delicious spicy sauce accented with pimento-filled olives and fresh cilantro enhances these swordfish steaks. The fish is marinated in a delicately tart sauce before grilling.

INGREDIENTS
(Serves 4)

- 1 garlic clove
- ¼ cup plus 2 tablespoons lime juice
- salt and pepper
- ⅓ cup olive oil
- 4 swordfish steaks (about 6 ounces *each*)

FOR THE SAUCE

- 1 pound ripe tomatoes
- 2 red serrano chiles or ¾ teaspoon crushed red pepper
- ⅓ cup pimento-filled green olives
- ¼ cup chopped fresh cilantro
- 1 tablespoon brown sugar
- 1 tablespoon white vinegar

INGREDIENT TIP

Both salmon and tuna are equally delicious here.

1 Prepare the marinade: Peel the garlic and pass through a garlic press into a large bowl. Whisk in ¼ cup of the lime juice, the olive oil, and ¼ teaspoon pepper. Add the swordfish, turning to coat. Set aside.

Step 1

2 Bring a large saucepan of water to a boil. Cut a cross into the root-end of each tomato. Lower the tomatoes into the boiling water for 1 minute. Remove with a slotted spoon, then plunge into a bowl of cold water to cool. Peel, then seed, the tomatoes. Pulse in a food processor to coarsely puree.

3 Seed and mince the serranos. Finely dice the olives; stir both into the tomato puree with the remaining 2 tablespoons lime juice, the cilantro, brown sugar, vinegar, and ¾ teaspoon salt. Prepare the grill.

Step 3

4 Remove the swordfish steaks from the marinade and place on the hot grill. Cook, turning once, until the fish is firm and only slightly pink in the center, about 6 minutes. Serve with the salsa.

Step 4

Preparation: 35 minutes
Grilling: 6 minutes
Per serving: 318 cal; 31 g pro; 17 g fat; 10 g carb.

TYPICALLY CARIBBEAN

Luxuriant vegetation thrives in the subtropical climate of the cluster of Caribbean islands. Chile peppers grow especially well in the hot, humid environment and are used frequently in the regional cuisine.

COOKING TIP

If your sauce turns out a bit too spicy, place a small bowl of brown sugar on the table to sprinkle on the food. Sugar offers some relief from the heat, which is why many tropical dishes are prepared from the start with a mixture of sweet and fiery ingredients.

SERVING TIPS

A side dish of curried onions and plantains is the perfect accompaniment here.

 A glass of Cuba Libre—white rum with cola, lemon juice, and lots of ice—is always refreshing.

STEAK MEXICANA

MEXICO

Any barbecue party will be a hit with a meal of chile-stuffed steaks and buttery corn. This unbeatable combination marries some of the most popular ingredients in Mexican cuisine.

INGREDIENTS
(Serves 4)

- 1 tablespoon *each* coriander seed and black peppercorns
- ¼ cup plus 2 tablespoons oil
- 4 garlic cloves, minced
- 1 tablespoon dried oregano
- 1 teaspoon ground cumin
- salt and pepper
- 5 serrano chiles
- 2 sirloin or filet mignon steaks or boneless pork chops (2 inches thick and about 12 ounces *each*)

IN ADDITION

- 4 fresh ears of corn
- 4 tablespoons butter, softened
- tortilla chips for serving

1 Prepare the grill. In a mortar or blender, coarsely grind the coriander seeds and black peppercorns. Place in a small bowl with ¼ cup of the oil, the garlic, oregano, cumin, and ¼ teaspoon salt. Stir until well blended.

2 Split and seed the chiles. Finely chop 1 chile; stir into the oil mixture. Flatten the steaks slightly, then cut a pocket into the side of each, taking care not to cut through the other side. Place the oil mixture and 2 chile halves in each pocket. Rub the remaining 2 tablespoons oil on the outside of both steaks. Set aside on a plate.

3 Husk and trim the corn. Brush 4 sheets of aluminum foil with the butter. Place an ear of corn on each, season with salt and pepper and wrap snugly. Grill them, while turning, for about 20 minutes.

4 After the corn has cooked for 5 minutes, add the steaks and grill for about 12 minutes, turning once, for medium-rare or until pork is cooked through. Let the steaks rest for 5 minutes, then cut each in half. Serve with the corn and tortilla chips.

Step 2

Step 2

Step 3

Preparation: 35 minutes
Grilling: 20 minutes
Per serving: 674 cal; 36 g pro; 51 g fat; 21 g carb.

TYPICALLY MEXICAN
Corn has been a mainstay of the Mexican diet since prehistoric times. Even the leaves of the plants are put to use, as numerous dishes are prepared in their husks.

COOKING TIP

The cooking time for the meat will depend on the thickness. For this dish, look for steaks or boneless chops which are about 4 inches in diameter and at least 2 inches thick.

SERVING TIPS

Round out your barbecue party with a white bean salad, guacamole, and crusty bread.

 Mexican beer, or a fruit-juice spritzer, is an excellent thirst quencher with this meal.

SESAME BEEF KABOBS

KOREA

In Korea, this dish is called "bulgogi." Thin slices of beef, marinated in a spicy ginger-sesame sauce, are skewered and then grilled tableside.

INGREDIENTS
(Serves 4)

- 2-pound piece beef tenderloin
- 1 bunch of scallions
- 2 garlic cloves
- 1-inch piece of fresh ginger
- 1 red Thai bird chile or ½ teaspoon crushed red pepper flakes
- ½ cup soy sauce
- 1 tablespoon honey
- 1 teaspoon vegetable oil
- 1 teaspoon Asian sesame oil
- ½ teaspoon black pepper

IN ADDITION
- 3 tablespoons sesame seeds

INGREDIENT TIP

If you can't get the beef tenderloin, use 2 pounds of filets mignons or flank steaks.

1 Cut the meat into ¼-inch-thick slices. Trim the root and tough green portion from the scallions and finely chop the remainder. Peel and chop the garlic and ginger. Place the scallions, garlic, and ginger in a shallow bowl.

2 Seed, devein, and finely chop the chile and add to the scallion mixture. Wash your hands immediately to avoid getting the hot chile oil in your eyes and on your skin.

3 Add ½ cup water, the soy sauce, honey, vegetable oil, sesame oil, and black pepper to the scallion mixture and stir until blended. Add the beef strips and turn to coat. Cover with foil and let marinate in the refrigerator for 3 hours.

4 Prepare the grill. Drain the beef slices, fold each in half, and thread securely onto skewers. Grill for 5–8 minutes, turning frequently with tongs.

5 While the meat cooks, roast the sesame seeds in a dry skillet over medium heat until toasted. Sprinkle the seeds over the kabobs before serving.

Step 1

Step 3

Step 4

Preparation: 50 minutes
Marinating: 3 hours
Grilling: 8 minutes
Per serving: 524 cal; 41 g pro; 35 g fat; 8 g carb.

TYPICALLY KOREAN
Whether as a seed or an oil, sesame adds a strong, nutty finishing touch to many Korean dishes. Though native to India, sesame flavoring was also used by the ancient Greeks and Egyptians.

COOKING TIPS

• Sesame seeds release their full flavor and aroma when they're roasted in a dry pan.

• If you let the meat marinate overnight, it will take on a particularly strong flavor.

• Soak wood or bamboo skewers in water about 20 minutes before using to keep them from burning.

SERVING TIPS

Try a cucumber salad seasoned with scallions, ginger, pepper, garlic, soy sauce, and sesame seeds.

It's customary to drink beer with this dish.
Iced tea also goes well.

SERVING TIPS Offer wasabi, a spicy seasoning paste, stirred into soy sauce as a dipping sauce.

In the summer, serve an ice-cold rice wine. Lightly warmed sake is a good wintertime choice.

TURKEY AND ASPARAGUS SKEWERS

JAPAN

Here's a treat for all fans of light cuisine —chunks of tender white turkey breast combined with green asparagus and crisp scallions. These skewers make perfect outdoor party fare.

INGREDIENTS
(Serves 4)

- 1 pound turkey breast

FOR THE MARINADE
- ½ cup rice wine or sherry
- ¼ cup soy sauce
- 1 tablespoon vegetable oil
- 1 teaspoon sugar

IN ADDITION
- 8 spears green asparagus
- 4 scallions

INGREDIENT TIPS
- The delicately sweet rice wine called mirin is a staple item in Japanese cooking.
- Instead of asparagus, you can use zucchini, which you will not have to precook.

1 Cut the turkey into 1-inch cubes. Place the rice wine, soy sauce, oil, and sugar in a shallow bowl and mix until the sugar dissolves. Add the turkey to the marinade. Toss to coat. Cover with foil and refrigerate for at least 2 hours.

Step 1

2 Meanwhile, remove the tough portions from the ends of the asparagus. Peel the lower third of each spear with a vegetable peeler. Blanch the asparagus in a saucepan of boiling salted water for 2 minutes, until crisp-tender. Drain and rinse with cold water until cool. Cut each spear into 3 pieces.

Step 2

3 Trim the roots and tough green portions from the scallions and quarter the remaining parts. Alternately arrange the pieces of asparagus, scallions, and turkey on skewers, making sure not to pack them too closely together.

4 Prepare the grill. Brush the kabobs with the marinade. Grill the kabobs for 15 minutes, turning frequently, until the turkey is cooked through.

Step 4

Preparation: 10 minutes
Marinating: 2 hours
Grilling: 15 minutes
Per serving: 209 cal; 30 g pro;
3 g fat; 8 g carb.

TYPICALLY JAPANESE
Marinades are one of the foundations of Japanese cuisine. The basic element is always soy sauce, which was introduced from China. In contrast to the Chinese, the Japanese prefer a lighter, milder variety of soy sauce.

TOKYO-STYLE STEAK

JAPAN

Here's a fragrant delicacy from the land of the rising sun. A refined marinade of soy sauce, plum sauce, and sherry gives the thin strips of beef a wonderful flavor.

INGREDIENTS

(Serves 4)

- 1½ pounds beef tenderloin or flank steak

FOR THE MARINADE
- 2-inch piece fresh ginger
- 2 garlic cloves
- a pinch of sugar
- 5 tablespoons Japanese soy sauce
- 5 tablespoons plum sauce
- 3 tablespoons mirin (sweet rice wine) or sherry

FOR THE SALAD
- 3 tablespoons rice wine vinegar
- 1 tablespoon sugar
- a pinch of salt
- 1 cucumber

INGREDIENT TIP

You can substitute Chinese soy sauce for the lighter, milder Japanese version— the stronger flavor won't overpower the beef.

1 Slice the meat into ¼-inch-thick slices. Peel and finely grate the ginger. Place half in a shallow bowl and the other half in a medium bowl. Peel the garlic and crush to a paste with a pinch of sugar.

2 Stir the garlic, soy sauce, plum sauce, and mirin into the ginger in the shallow bowl. Add the meat, and toss to coat. Cover and refrigerate for 30 minutes.

Step 1

3 Add the vinegar, sugar, salt, and 2 table- spoons of water to the ginger in the medium bowl. Stir until the sugar and salt dissolve. Peel the cucumber and slice in half lengthwise. Scoop out the seeds with a spoon, cut the halves crosswise into thin slices, and add to the ginger. Toss to coat. Cover and refrigerate for at least 30 minutes.

Step 3

4 Prepare the grill. Skewer the beef using 2 skewers for each slice to keep it flat. Cook for 1½–2 minutes, turning frequently.

5 Distribute the cucumber salad onto 4 plates. Remove the beef slices from the skewers and arrange them next to the salad.

Step 4

Preparation: 30 minutes
Marinating: 30 minutes
Grilling: 2 minutes
Per serving: 424 cal; 31 g pro; 23 g fat; 18 g carb.

TYPICALLY JAPANESE

Ceremonial events in Japan often involve food and drink. A classic example is the tea ceremony. During the ritual, the host prepares a green tea, which is served with charac- teristic spiritual peace and harmony.

COOKING TIP

In one popular variation, the grilled beef slices are served with a delicious sauce. For this, double the amount of marinade. After marinating the steaks, bring the leftover marinade to a boil in a saucepan. Mix 1 teaspoon cornstarch with water and stir into the marinade. Cook, stirring, until the sauce is clear.

SERVING TIPS

Besides wasabi (spicy green paste), offer pickled ginger, seaweed salad, and oyster sauce as accompaniments.

 Drink green tea, cold Japanese beer, or warm sake with your meal.

TANDOORI CHICKEN SKEWERS

INDIA

INGREDIENTS
(Serves 4)

- 1½ pounds skinless boneless chicken breasts
- ½ cup lime juice
- salt and black pepper

FOR THE MARINADE
- 1 jalapeño chile
- 1 onion
- 2 garlic cloves
- 1-inch piece of fresh ginger
- 2 cups plain yogurt
- 1 tablespoon vegetable oil
- 1 tablespoon curry powder
- pinch of saffron threads (optional)

INGREDIENT TIP
After handling the jalapeño or any other chile, wash your hands immediately to avoid getting the hot chile oil in your eyes and on your skin.

Hardly anyone can resist the scent of Indian spices—especially enticing when mixed with the aroma of chicken roasting on a grill. Here, yogurt and lime juice offer tangy tastes.

1 Rinse the chicken in cold water, pat dry with paper towels, and cut into thin strips. Place the chicken pieces in a medium bowl and sprinkle with half of the lime juice, 1 teaspoon salt, and ½ teaspoon black pepper. Toss to coat. Cover with foil and refrigerate while preparing the marinade.

Step 1

2 Seed, devein, and finely chop the jalapeño and place in a large bowl. Peel and grate the onion. Peel the garlic and crush to a paste with a pinch of salt. Peel and chop the ginger. Add the onion, garlic, ginger, yogurt, oil, curry powder, saffron, and the remaining lime juice to the jalapeño. Whisk until blended.

Step 3

3 Thread the chicken pieces onto 8 skewers and place in a shallow dish. Pour the yogurt mixture over the skewers, cover, and refrigerate for 4 hours.

4 Prepare the grill. Remove the chicken skewers from the yogurt mixture, and pat lightly with paper towels. Cover the grill rack with foil. Grill the chicken for 10–15 minutes, turning the skewers frequently.

Step 4

Preparation: 35 minutes
Marinating: 4 hours
Grilling: 15 minutes
Per serving: 258 cal; 43 g pro; 5 g fat; 9 g carb.

TYPICALLY INDIAN
Indians grill and bake many dishes in a special oven called a tandoor, which is tall and cylindrical and made of brick and clay. Well-seasoned chunks of beef or chicken are skewered and cooked quickly in the glowing fire.

COOKING TIP

Create your own curry powder. Using a blender, grind together 1 tablespoon *each* cloves, cumin seed, cardamom seeds, and black peppercorns. Combine this with 1 tablespoon *each* ground nutmeg and ground cinnamon. Store in an airtight container.

SERVING TIPS

Pappadams (crispy lentil flatbreads) and cumin-flavored yogurt complete the grilled chicken meal.

 Ice water is obligatory at any Indian meal. You can also serve sweetened iced tea.

$\mathcal{S}$AVORY MEATBALL KABOBS

JORDAN

Grilling gives these exotically spiced meatballs a delightfully rich flavor. This quick-cooking Middle Eastern specialty will delight young and old alike.

INGREDIENTS
(Serves 4)

- 1½ pounds ground lamb
- 1 onion
- 1 cup bread crumbs
- 1 egg
- 1 teaspoon garlic salt
- 1 teaspoon dried thyme
- ½ teaspoon ground cumin
- salt and pepper
- 6 tablespoons olive oil

FOR THE SAUCE
- 1 bunch of flat-leaf parsley
- 1 cup yogurt
- 1 tablespoon lemon juice
- pinch of saffron threads

IN ADDITION
- 4 lemons

INGREDIENT TIPS

- For a rich, sumptuous sauce, use whole-milk yogurt, not the low-fat variety.
- You can use ground beef instead of ground lamb.

1 Place the lamb in a large bowl. Peel and grate the onion. Add the onion, bread crumbs, egg, garlic salt, thyme, cumin, ¾ teaspoon salt, and ½ teaspoon pepper to the lamb. Mix well. With wet hands, shape the mixture into 32 equal-size balls.

2 Thread 4 meatballs onto each of 8 skewers. Place on a plate, brush with the oil, cover with foil, and refrigerate for 1 hour.

3 Meanwhile, rinse and dry the parsley. Pick ½ cup leaves, finely chop, and place in a medium bowl. Add the yogurt, lemon juice, saffron, and ¼ teaspoon *each* salt and pepper. Cover and refrigerate.

4 Prepare the grill. Grill the skewers for 8–10 minutes, turning frequently, until the meatballs are cooked through and browned on all sides.

5 Slice the lemons and spread out the slices on 4 plates. Top each with 2 of the skewers and garnish with a parsley sprig. Serve with the sauce.

Step 1

Step 2

Step 3

Preparation: 30 minutes
Chilling: 1 hour
Grilling: 10 minutes
Per serving: 695 cal; 38 g pro; 47 g fat; 29 g carb.

TYPICALLY JORDANIAN
In numerous restaurants in Jordan, one can feast on kabob—cubed lamb grilled with colorful vegetables on long skewers. Grilled skewered meatballs are also traditional Jordanian fare.

COOKING TIP

Grill the meatballs on the rack for a few minutes to brown the meatballs and give them a crispy exterior before covering the rack with foil. Do not overcook them; lamb tastes better and is moister when cooked no more than to medium doneness.

SERVING TIPS

Appropriate side dishes include a variety of olives, steamed okra, and unleavened bread.

 You can serve ice water with a splash of lemon or offer cold peppermint tea.

GRILLED LEMONY CHICKEN

LEBANON

Tender pieces of chicken are marinated in lemon, thyme, and parsley, then grilled. Hummus is served alongside, a Middle Eastern dip made of ground chickpeas and sesame seeds.

INGREDIENTS
(Serves 6)

- two 3-pound chickens

FOR THE MARINADE
- 4 garlic cloves
- salt and pepper
- 1 cup lemon juice
- ¼ cup plus 2 tablespoons olive oil
- ¼ cup chopped parsley plus sprigs for garnish
- 1 teaspoon dried thyme

FOR THE DIP
- 1 can (19 ounces) chickpeas
- ½ cup sesame tahini
- 1 teaspoon ground cumin

IN ADDITION
- lemon wedges

INGREDIENT TIP
Tahini is a paste of ground sesame seeds. It's available at large supermarkets or Middle Eastern grocery stores.

1 Rinse the chickens in cold water and pat dry with paper towels. Cut each chicken into 4 pieces; place in a shallow baking dish.

2 Peel the garlic. Crush 2 cloves to a paste with a pinch of salt. Place the garlic in a small bowl. Add ½ cup lemon juice, ¼ cup oil, the chopped parsley, and the thyme; mix well. Brush the garlic marinade over the chicken, cover, and refrigerate for 1 hour.

3 Drain and rinse the chickpeas and place in a food processor. Add the remaining 2 garlic cloves and ½ cup lemon juice, the tahini, cumin, and ½ teaspoon *each* salt and pepper. Process until the mixture is a thick puree, adding 2–3 tablespoons warm water to make the mixture a dipping consistency. Place in a serving bowl.

4 Prepare the grill. Cook the chicken for 20–25 minutes, turning frequently, until the juices run clear when it is pierced and an instant-read thermometer inserted at the thickest portion registers 160°F.

5 Place the chicken on plates and garnish with parsley sprigs and lemon wedges. Serve the hummus on the side.

Step 1

Step 2

Step 3

Preparation: 25 minutes
Marinating: 1 hour
Grilling: 25 minutes
Per serving: 750 cal; 62 g pro;
49 g fat; 16 g carb.

TYPICALLY LEBANESE
In the Middle East, bread accompanies nearly every meal. Early in the day, bakers begin mixing and rolling out dough to make the oven-fresh goods. Pita bread makes a wonderful accompaniment to hummus.

COOKING TIP

If you can find only dried chickpeas, soak them overnight in enough water to cover by a few inches. Simmer, covered, in the same water over low heat for 1 hour.

SERVING TIPS

Combine 2 cups couscous with 1 cup hot broth. Let soak. Stir in raisins, almonds, and parsley.

 Serve iced or hot peppermint tea made with fresh mint. Garnish with sliced lemon.

ℱRAGRANT LAMB KABOBS

TURKEY

The tender chunks of lamb on these skewers are first placed in an olive-oil marinade seasoned with a pinch of cinnamon. Then they're grilled until browned and served with rice.

INGREDIENTS
(Serves 4)

- 2 pounds boneless lamb shoulder

FOR THE MARINADE
- 2 large onions
- 2 large lemons
- 1 garlic clove
- salt and black pepper
- 2 bay leaves
- ½ cup olive oil
- 2 teaspoons dried thyme
- ½ teaspoon cayenne pepper
- ¼ teaspoon cinnamon

INGREDIENT TIP
To save time, you can ask your butcher to cut the lamb shoulder into cubes.

1 Cut the meat into 1½-inch cubes without removing the fat and set aside. Peel the onions and grate into a large bowl. (Or use a food processor to puree the onions.) Grate the lemon peels and place in the same bowl; squeeze in the juice.

2 Peel the garlic and pass through a garlic press into the onion marinade. Chop or crush the bay leaves. Add the garlic, bay leaves, oil, thyme, 1 teaspoon salt, ½ teaspoon black pepper, the cayenne pepper, and cinnamon to the marinade and mix well.

3 Add the lamb cubes to the onion marinade. Mix together well, cover with plastic wrap, and refrigerate for 4 hours.

4 Prepare the grill. Skewer the lamb cubes onto 4 long metal skewers. Cook for about 6–8 minutes, turning the skewers frequently with tongs. Do not overcook.

Step 1

Step 3

Step 4

Preparation: 30 minutes
Marinating: 4 hours
Grilling: 8 minutes
Per serving: 731 cal; 40 g pro; 57 g fat; 14 g carb.

TYPICALLY TURKISH
A kabob in Turkey can mean a variety of meat, fish, or vegetables, typically marinated, skewered, and grilled over coals. These succulent skewers are popular throughout the country.

COOKING TIP

Remove the tough sinews and gristle when preparing the lamb. However, take care not to remove the fat, which ensures that the meat will stay juicy while it cooks. For this reason, it's best to alternate lean and fatty pieces of meat when threading the skewers.

SERVING TIPS

On the side, offer pickled peppers, pita bread or rice, and a bowl of plain yogurt as a simple, zesty sauce.

 Ayran—a Turkish drink made of yogurt, water, and either sugar or salt—is very refreshing.

SERVING TIPS Complete this meal with a Greek country salad accented with olives and feta cheese.

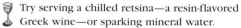 Try serving a chilled retsina—a resin-flavored Greek wine—or sparking mineral water.

ℒEMON-ROSEMARY CHICKEN

GREECE

On the Greek island of Crete, you might find a tangy lemon chicken like this one, which is grilled until crisp and juicy. Fresh rosemary makes this dish incomparably tasty.

INGREDIENTS
(Serves 6)

- two 3-pound chickens

FOR THE MARINADE
- 2 large shallots
- 6 garlic cloves
- 8 long fresh rosemary sprigs
- 6 tablespoons lemon juice
- ½ cup olive oil

FOR THE ROSEMARY BUTTER
- 1 stick (8 tablespoons) butter at room temperature
- 3 tablespoons lemon juice
- salt and pepper

IN ADDITION
- lemon wedges

INGREDIENT TIPS

- To save time, buy chicken breasts or leg quarters.
- Rosemary is easy to grow as a potted plant on a balcony or sunny windowsill.

1 Rinse the chickens in cold water and pat dry with paper towels. Cut each chicken into 4 pieces and set aside.

2 Peel and slice the shallots and garlic and place in a shallow baking dish. Remove enough of the needles from the rosemary sprigs to make 1 cup; finely chop. Reserve the remaining sprigs. Add half the chopped rosemary, 6 tablespoons lemon juice, and the oil to the shallot mixture and mix well.

3 Place the chicken pieces in the shallot marinade. Turn to coat. Cover with plastic wrap and refrigerate for 2 hours.

4 In a small bowl, whisk the butter, remaining chopped rosemary, 3 tablespoons lemon juice, and ½ teaspoon *each* salt and pepper until smooth. Place in a serving bowl and refrigerate.

5 Prepare the grill. Drain the chicken and cook for 20–30 minutes, turning the pieces frequently. Place the chicken on plates and garnish with rosemary sprigs and lemon wedges. Serve with the lemon-rosemary butter on the side.

Step 1

Step 3

Step 4

Preparation: 30 minutes
Marinating: 2 hours
Grilling: 20–30 minutes
Per serving: 705 cal; 55 g pro;
52 g fat; 3 g carb.

TYPICALLY GREEK
The ancient Greeks roasted their chickens whole over an outdoor fire. Even today, modern Greeks often roast meat outside, and the meal is shared with friends, relatives, or neighbors.

TUNA STEAK WITH CAPER SAUCE

PORTUGAL

Here's a special dish from Portugal—spicy grilled tuna steaks accompanied by a zesty mayonnaise-based sauce that's flavored with capers and lemon juice.

INGREDIENTS

(Serves 4)

- 4 fresh tuna steaks (6 ounces *each*)

FOR THE MARINADE

- 1 red serrano chile
- 2 garlic cloves
- 1 rosemary sprig
- ¼ cup chopped parsley
- 1 lemon
- ½ cup olive oil
- 3 tablespoons orange juice
- 10 black peppercorns
- 2 bay leaves

FOR THE MAYONNAISE

- 1 jar (6 ounces) capers
- 1 lemon
- ½ cup mayonnaise
- 1 tablespoon anchovy paste (optional)
- black pepper

INGREDIENT TIP

Anchovy paste is very strongly flavored. If you omit it, add ¼ teaspoon salt to the sauce.

1 Place the tuna steaks in a shallow baking dish. Seed, devein, and finely chop the chile and place in a small bowl. Peel and chop the garlic. Remove the needles from the rosemary and finely chop. Add the garlic, rosemary, and parsley to the chile. Squeeze the juice from 1 lemon into the chile mixture. Add the oil, orange juice, peppercorns, and bay leaves and mix well.

Step 1

2 Add the chile marinade to the dish with the tuna and turn the fish to coat. Cover with plastic wrap and refrigerate for 2 hours.

3 Prepare the grill. Drain the capers. Grate 1 teaspoon peel from the remaining lemon into a small bowl and squeeze in the juice. Add the capers, mayonnaise, anchovy paste, and ¼ teaspoon black pepper. Whisk until blended and smooth.

Step 2

4 Drain the fish and grill for 8 minutes, turning the steaks over with a spatula after 4 minutes. Serve with the caper sauce.

Step 3

Preparation: 20 minutes
Marinating: 2 hours
Grilling: 8 minutes
Per serving: 587 cal; 40 g pro; 44 g fat; 7 g carb.

TYPICALLY PORTUGUESE

Since ancient times, tuna has been harvested in the waters surrounding Portugal during the fish's biannual migrations to and from the region.

COOKING TIP

Tuna is superb for grilling. The delectably seared outer layer keeps the inner portion of the steak juicy. Pay special attention to the suggested cooking time: If you grill the fish too long, the outside will become tough and leathery and the inner part will be too dry.

SERVING TIPS

Wrap portions of cooked rice mixed with garlic, salt, and pepper in foil packets; heat with the fish.

 Offer the famous Portuguese Vinho Verde, which means "green wine."

CRISPY CHICKEN WITH RED SAUCE

SPAIN

INGREDIENTS
(Serves 4)

- 8 chicken leg quarters
- 3 fresh thyme sprigs

FOR THE RED SAUCE

- 1 red serrano chile
- 1 pound tomatoes
- 2 tablespoons olive oil
- 3 garlic cloves
- ¼ cup sherry vinegar
- salt and black pepper

FOR THE BASTING SAUCE

- 6 tablespoons olive oil
- ⅓ cup honey
- 2 tablespoons sherry vinegar
- 2 tablespoons sherry
- 1 garlic clove

INGREDIENT TIP

For a particularly zesty taste, grate a hearty, flavorful dry cheese—such as the Spanish Manchego—into the tomato sauce just before serving.

Based on a traditional Spanish recipe, this simple yet truly delicious dish features chicken quarters marinated in an aromatic mixture of sherry and honey.

1 Rinse the chicken in cold water and pat dry with paper towels. Remove the thyme leaves from the stems, chop, and rub into the leg quarters.

2 Seed, devein, and finely chop the chile. Coarsely chop the tomatoes. Heat 2 tablespoons olive oil in a large skillet over medium heat. Peel and crush 3 garlic cloves through a garlic press into the oil. Add the chile and sauté for 1 minute. Add the tomatoes and cook for 10 minutes.

3 Pass the tomatoes through a sieve into a medium saucepan. Stir in ¼ cup sherry vinegar, ¼ teaspoon salt, and a pinch of black pepper. Keep warm over low heat.

4 Prepare the grill. In a small bowl, combine 6 tablespoons olive oil, the honey, 2 tablespoons sherry vinegar, and the sherry. Peel 1 garlic clove and crush through a garlic press into the oil mixture. Mix well.

5 Grill the chicken for 20–30 minutes, turning the pieces frequently and brushing with the basting sauce. Serve with the red sauce.

Step 1

Step 3

Step 4

Preparation: 40 minutes
Grilling: 20–30 minutes
Per serving: 891 cal; 61 g pro; 58 g fat; 32 g carb.

TYPICALLY SPANISH

Spain is heaven for tomato lovers. On farms and experimental plantations, growers cultivate the succulent fruits, often striving for diversity through new hybrid technology.

COOKING TIP

While the chicken is cooking, use a spatula or tongs to turn it. Don't poke into the meat with a fork—if the meat loses juice, it will dry out.

SERVING TIPS

Tapas—small appetizers such as anchovies, mushrooms, and almonds—enliven the dinner.

In keeping with tradition, serve Rioja wine or sangria, the famous wine-and-fruit punch.

SERVING TIPS Accompany your vegetables with grilled sausages or pork chops and a baguette.

A pleasant pairing for this dish is a light, well-chilled rosé from Provence.

$\mathcal{P}$ROVENÇAL GRILLED VEGETABLES

FRANCE

The mouthwatering aroma as this bright, colorful marinated vegetable medley cooks on the grill will entice your guests. The dish also makes a beautiful presentation at the table.

INGREDIENTS
(Serves 4)

FOR THE DIPPING SAUCE
- 2 garlic cloves
- ¼ cup orange juice
- 1½ tablespoons Dijon mustard
- 1 tablespoon lime juice
- 1 teaspoon ground coriander
- salt and pepper
- ½ cup olive oil

FOR THE VEGETABLES
- 1 can (14 ounces) artichoke hearts
- 1 green bell pepper
- 1 red bell pepper
- ¾ pound oyster, shiitake, or large white mushrooms
- 1 large zucchini
- 1 small eggplant
- 8 bacon strips
- ¾ pound green beans

1 For the dipping sauce, peel the garlic and pass through a garlic press into a small bowl. Add the orange juice, mustard, lime juice, coriander, ¼ teaspoon salt, and ⅛ teaspoon pepper. Whisk in oil.

Step 1

2 Bring a large pot of salted water to a boil. Preheat the oven to 350°F. Cut the artichoke hearts lengthwise in half. Slice the bell peppers in half, remove the seeds and veins, and quarter them lengthwise. Clean the oyster mushrooms and cut any large ones in half. Wash and trim the zucchini and eggplant and cut them into ½-inch slices.

Step 2

3 In a large skillet over medium heat, sauté the bacon for 5 minutes, until it is half-cooked (do not let it get crisp). Trim the beans and add to the boiling water; cook for 5–7 minutes, until just tender. Drain the beans and divide them into 4 portions. Wrap up each portion with 2 slices of bacon and secure with toothpicks. Prepare the grill.

Step 3

4 Brush the vegetables with a quarter of the dipping sauce and season with ½ teaspoon salt and ¼ teaspoon pepper. Grill them for 10–15 minutes. Serve with the remaining dipping sauce on the side.

Preparation: 50 minutes
Grilling: 15 minutes
Per serving: 442 cal; 11 g pro; 34 g fat; 27 g carb.

TYPICALLY FRENCH
The French know how to appreciate simple pleasures, like a quiet outdoor game of *boule*. Such simplicity is equally important at the table, where the earthy, garlic-laced Provençal mayonnaise, aïoli, frequently accompanies fish, meats, and, as above, fresh vegetables.

NUT-CRUSTED LAMB CHOPS

FRANCE

Create a wonderful barbecue meal in the Southern French style—tender flame-seared lamb chops nestled in a delicious hazelnut crust and served with herb-buttered potatoes.

INGREDIENTS
(Serves 8)

- 8 (1½-inch-thick) leg lamb chops (7 ounces *each*)
- salt and pepper
- 7 tablespoons olive oil
- 2 tablespoons herbes de Provence
- 2 pounds all-purpose potatoes, boiled the day before

FOR THE BUTTER

- ½ cup chopped hazelnuts
- 1 stick (4 ounces) butter, at room temperature

IN ADDITION

- 2 tablespoons watercress or radish sprouts

INGREDIENT TIP

The French consider herbes de Provence—a fragrant mixture of rosemary, thyme, bay leaves, sweet basil, and savory—especially suitable for grilled foods.

1 Flatten the lamb chops with a meat mallet. Sprinkle with ½ teaspoon salt and ¼ teaspoon pepper. In a small bowl, combine the olive oil and herbs and brush half of the mixture over the lamb chops.

2 Brush 8 sheets of aluminum foil with the remaining herb oil. Peel the boiled potatoes, thinly slice, and place in a large bowl. Sprinkle with ¼ teaspoon *each* salt and pepper and toss gently. Divide the potatoes among the sheets of foil, fold up the edges of the foil, and seal.

3 Prepare the grill. Place the nuts in a dry skillet and roast over medium heat until toasted. Let cool. In a small bowl, mix the butter with the hazelnuts and watercress.

4 Place the lamb chops and the potato packets on the grill. Grill the chops for 8–10 minutes, until their coating is crisp.

5 As soon as the lamb chops are grilled on both sides, spread one side with hazelnut butter and broil it on the top. Serve the potatoes along with the meat.

Step 1

Step 2

Step 3

Preparation: 30 minutes
Grilling: 10 minutes
Per serving: 674 cal; 30 g pro; 52 g fat; 22 g carb.

TYPICALLY FRENCH

The French commonly end a meal with cheese, and their country is truly unique in its almost endless variety of cheeses. No other nation in the world comes close to matching its more than 600 distinct types.

COOKING TIPS

• The butter should be spread onto the lamb chops only at the end of the cooking time. Otherwise, the nuts may burn too quickly and become bitter.

• If you prefer not to broil the butter mixture on top of the chops, just serve it on the side. That way, your guests can help themselves.

SERVING TIPS

Try stuffing a tomato with chunks of goat cheese, then drizzle with olive oil and cook on the grill.

A Beaujolais goes excellently with this dish.
As an aperitif, offer pastis, the aniseed liqueur.

$\mathscr{S}$HRIMP AND GARLIC SKEWERS

ITALY

This special seafood dish hails from the Italian region of Liguria, where it's known as "gamberoni allo spiedo." Whole cloves of garlic give the skewered shrimp its distinctive taste.

INGREDIENTS

(Serves 8)

- 16 large shrimp
- 2½ tablespoons lemon juice
- 12 garlic cloves
- salt and pepper

FOR THE MAYONNAISE

- 2 garlic cloves
- 2 tablespoons pine nuts
- 2 anchovy fillets
- ½ cup mayonnaise
- ½ cup chopped parsley
- 2½ tablespoons lemon juice
- 2 tablespoons capers

FOR THE BASTING SAUCE

- ¼ cup plus 2 tablespoons olive oil
- 2 tablespoons chopped fresh basil
- 1 tablespoon tomato paste

IN ADDITION

- lemon wedges

1 Peel and devein the shrimp, leaving the tails intact. Rinse in cold water and place in a medium bowl. Sprinkle with 2½ tablespoons lemon juice and ½ teaspoon *each* salt and pepper and toss to mix. Place 12 garlic cloves in a small saucepan with 1 cup of water. Heat to boiling and simmer for 15 minutes; drain and peel the garlic.

Step 1

2 Prepare the grill. Peel and finely chop 2 garlic cloves and place in a medium bowl. Coarsely chop the pine nuts and finely chop the anchovies. Add the pine nuts, anchovies, the mayonnaise, parsley, 2½ tablespoons lemon juice, capers, and ½ teaspoon *each* salt and pepper to the garlic and mix well.

Step 3

3 Alternately arrange 4 shrimp and 3 parboiled garlic cloves on each of 4 skewers. In a cup, mix the olive oil, basil, and tomato paste and brush the mixture over the skewered shrimp and garlic.

Step 4

4 Grill the shrimp and garlic for 6 minutes, frequently turning the skewers and brushing repeatedly with the basil oil. Garnish with the lemon wedges and serve the mayonnaise on the side.

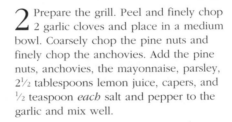

Preparation: 45 minutes
Grilling: 6 minutes
Per serving: 474 cal; 11 g pro; 45 g fat; 8 g carb.

TYPICALLY LIGURIAN

Situated between the picturesque Alps and the rocky cliffs of the Mediterranean coast, the Liguria region of northwest Italy is known for its bountiful supply and its people's creative use of aromatic herbs.

COOKING TIP

For a quick soup, sauté the shrimp shells with
2 cloves chopped garlic and 1 tablespoon tomato
paste. Add 1 cup Prosecco or other dry white wine,
⅓ cup Marsala, and ½ cup water. Let simmer for
15 minutes. Pour through a sieve, stir in 1 cup cream,
heat, and season to taste.

SERVING TIPS

Perfect complements to the meal
are flat bread and a green salad
tossed with balsamic vinaigrette.

Enjoy a dry Italian red wine, such as Barbaresco
or Barolo, or a crisp white Pinot Grigio.

HERBED PORK CHOPS

Finely chopped Mediterranean herbs, fresh from the garden or marketplace, enhance this succulent entree. Tangy olive butter adds a creamy nuance.

INGREDIENTS

(Serves 4)

- 1 shallot
- 2 bay leaves
- ½ cup olive oil
- ¼ cup mixed chopped fresh herbs—thyme, sage, oregano, rosemary, basil
- 3 tablespoons lemon juice
- 1 teaspoon fennel seeds
- 4 (1-inch-thick) pork chops (6 ounces *each*)

FOR THE BUTTER
- 1 cup black olives, pitted
- 2 garlic cloves
- salt and pepper
- 1 stick (8 tablespoons) butter, at room temperature

IN ADDITION
- lemon wedges, herb sprigs

INGREDIENT TIP
For authentic flavor, use imported olives, available in specialty grocery stores.

1 Peel and finely dice the shallot and place in a small bowl. Crush the bay leaves and add to the shallot. Add the olive oil, herbs, lemon juice, and fennel seeds.

2 Place the pork chops in a deep dish. Spread the shallot marinade on top. Cover with foil and refrigerate for 2 hours.

3 Prepare the grill. Finely chop the olives and place in a medium bowl. Peel the garlic and pass through a press. Add the garlic, butter, and a pinch of pepper to the olives and mix well. Place in a serving bowl, cover, and refrigerate.

4 Place the chops on the grill rack and grill for 5–6 minutes, turning the chops over after 3 minutes. Sprinkle with ½ teaspoon *each* salt and pepper. Garnish with lemon wedges and herbs. Serve with the olive butter.

Step 1

Step 2

Step 3

Preparation: 20 minutes
Marinating: 2 hours
Grilling: 6 minutes
Per serving: 834 cal; 24 g pro; 81 g fat; 5 g carb.

TYPICALLY ITALIAN
The mountainous central Italian region of Abruzzi seems to have been made for the cultivation of olives, the small green fruits that are so prized by cooks.

COOKING TIP

You can use the broiler to cook the pork chops instead of an outdoor barbecue grill if you desire. Preheat the broiler, place the chops on a rack in a broiler pan, and cook as directed in the recipe.

SERVING TIPS

Begin the meal with a pretty platter of goat cheese and marinated mixed vegetables.

🍷 Enjoy a glass of dry wine—either red or white—or a spritzer with your meal.

KABOBS—THREE WAYS

Skewers of tender, lean, bite-size morsels of meat are a real delight. Here are three delicious recipes that you can try on your grill.

SPICY LAMB SKEWERS

| Preparation: 30 minutes | Marinating: 6 hours | Grilling: 10 minutes |

SPAIN

(SERVES 4)

- 2 pounds lean boneless lamb (from the leg)
- 1 bunch of parsley
- 8 garlic cloves
- salt and black pepper
- 5 tablespoons lemon juice
- ½ teaspoon ground cumin
- ½ teaspoon paprika
- a pinch of cayenne pepper
- ¼ cup oil

1 Cut the meat into thin, 1-inch-wide strips. Rinse, dry, and chop the parsley and place in a large resealable plastic bag. Peel the garlic, and pass through a garlic press.

2 Add the garlic, black pepper, lemon juice, cumin, paprika, and cayenne to the parsley and squeeze the bag to mix. Add the lamb and squeeze to work the parsley marinade into the meat. Seal the bag and refrigerate for 6 hours, shaking the meat frequently.

3 Prepare the grill. Thread the meat onto wooden skewers so that each slice is pierced in 2 places. Brush the meat with the oil and grill for 8–10 minutes, turning the skewers frequently. Season with salt to taste.

MEAT AND

| Preparation: 25 minutes |

RUSSIA

(SERVES 4)

- 1½ pounds boneless lamb
- salt and black pepper
- 2 onions
- ¼ cup chopped parsley
- 1 teaspoon ground coriander
- 5 tablespoons vinegar
- ¼ cup oil
- 1 tablespoon lemon juice
- 1 cup mushrooms
- 1 red bell pepper
- 1 green bell pepper

1 Cut the lamb into 2-inch cubes. Peel the onions; chop one; place in a large resealable plastic bag.

BEEF SATAY

Preparation: 25 minutes   Marinating: 1 hour   Grilling: 8 minutes

THAILAND

(SERVES 4)

- 1½ pounds beef flank steak
- 3 jalapeño chiles
- 1-inch piece fresh ginger
- 5 tablespoons peanut oil
- 3 tablespoons soy sauce
- 1 teaspoon curry powder
- 1 onion
- 3 garlic cloves
- 1 cup unsalted peanuts
- ½ cup peanut butter
- ½ cup vegetable broth
- 1 tablespoon chopped fresh cilantro
- salt and black pepper

1 Cut the meat against the grain into thin slices. Seed, devein, and finely chop the chiles. Peel the ginger and finely chop. Place half the chiles, the ginger, 2 table-spoons oil, the soy sauce, and the curry powder in a large resealable plastic bag.

2 Squeeze the bag to mix. Add the beef; squeeze to work the chile marinade into the meat. Seal the bag; refrigerate for 1 hour.

3 Peel and finely chop the onion and garlic. Heat 2 tablespoons oil in a large skillet over medium heat. Sauté the onion for 3 minutes; add the remaining chiles and the garlic and sauté for 1 minute. Stir in the peanuts, peanut butter, broth, cilantro, and ¼ teaspoon *each* salt and black pepper.

4 Prepare the grill. Thread the meat strips onto skewers in zigzag fashion and brush with the remaining 1 tablespoon oil. Grill for 5-8 minutes, turning the skewers frequently. Serve with the peanut sauce.

VEGETABLE KABOBS

Marinating: 4 hours Grilling: 8 minutes

2 Add the parsley, coriander, vinegar, 2 table-spoons oil, and the lemon juice; squeeze the bag to mix. Add the lamb; squeeze to work marinade into the meat. Seal the bag; refrigerate for 4 hours, shaking the meat frequently.

3 Cut the other onion into 8 wedges. Clean the mush-rooms. Seed and devein the bell peppers; cut into 2-inch cubes. Prepare the grill.

4 Arrange the meat and vegetables on 4 skewers. Brush with the remaining oil. Grill, turning frequently, for 8 minutes.

PEPPERY STEAK AND CHEESY ZUCCHINI

With a spicy marinade, these steaks become tender and take on an extraordinary flavor. Just a few minutes on the grill, and this delicacy is ready to eat.

INGREDIENTS
(Serves 4)

FOR THE STEAKS
- 1 teaspoon black peppercorns
- 2 tablespoons olive oil
- ½ teaspoon paprika
- ¼ teaspoon Tabasco sauce
- 4 filets mignons (1½ inches thick)

FOR THE ZUCCHINI
- 2 zucchinis
- 1 tablespoon plus ⅓ cup olive oil
- salt and black pepper
- 2 ounces Parmesan cheese, grated

INGREDIENT TIPS

- Replace the filets mignons with extra-thick T-bone steaks or slices of pork tenderloin.
- You can use another grated hard cheese, such as Asiago or Romano, instead of the Parmesan.

1 Coarsely grind the peppercorns in a mortar or pepper mill and place in a small bowl. Add 2 tablespoons olive oil, the paprika, and Tabasco and mix well. Rub the mixture into the steaks. Cover with foil and refrigerate for 2 hours.

2 Prepare the grill. Cut the zucchini into ¼-inch-thick slices. Place in a broiling pan and brush with 1 tablespoon olive oil. Sprinkle with ¼ teaspoon *each* salt and black pepper. In a small bowl, mix the remaining ⅓ cup oil with the Parmesan.

3 Cook the steaks for 4–6 minutes on each side. After 4 minutes, place the zucchini on the grill rack with the steaks and cook for 2 minutes.

4 Turn the zucchini slices over and cook for 1 minute. Brush the slices with the Parmesan mixture and cook until the cheese begins to melt. Sprinkle the steaks with ½ teaspoon salt; serve the zucchini with the steaks.

Step 1

Step 2

Step 2

Preparation: 15 minutes
Marinating: 2 hours
Grilling: 12 minutes
Per serving: 660 cal; 36 g pro;
56 g fat; 4 g carb.

TYPICALLY GERMAN
At the height of summer in Germany, the flavorful aroma that wafts from countless gardens is a signal that the grilling season has begun. Accompaniments like sausages and potato salad are always on hand.

COOKING TIP

You might want to grill the zucchini on a sheet of aluminum foil with holes poked through it. This helps prevent the loss of any cheese into the fire.

SERVING TIPS

Every barbecue needs a rich assortment of breads, like country-style whole wheat and fresh rolls.

Beer, red wine, or sparkling red or white grape juice goes well here.

SERVING TIPS Boiled potatoes go very well with this dish. Serve them with just butter and salt.

 Offer a dry white wine or a tall glass of ice-cold beer to accompany the fish.

TENDER COD IN FOIL

GERMANY

INGREDIENTS
(Serves 4)

FOR THE FISH
- 2 tablespoons butter
- 2 tablespoons minced fresh chives
- 4 cod fillets (about 6 ounces *each*)
- ¼ cup white wine
- 2 tablespoons lemon juice
- salt and white pepper

FOR THE SPINACH
- 2 tablespoons butter
- 1½ pounds fresh spinach
- 1 onion
- 2 garlic cloves
- ¼ pound bacon strips

IN ADDITION
- lemon slices

INGREDIENT TIP
Excellent alternatives to the cod include mackerel, trout, red snapper, halibut, salmon, and flounder.

A succulent combination of cod, bacon, and spinach grills beautifully in an aluminum foil packet. Since the fish has so few calories, you can enjoy the bacon without guilt.

1 Prepare the grill. In a small bowl, mix 2 tablespoons butter with the chives and grease 4 sheets of foil with half the mixture. Place 1 fillet on each sheet of foil; spread some of the remaining chive butter on each fillet. Season with the wine, lemon juice, and a pinch of salt and white pepper Fold up the foil to make packets.

Step 1

2 Grease 4 more sheets of foil with butter. Rinse the spinach, pat dry, and trim off the tough stems. Place a quarter of the spinach onto each sheet of foil.

3 Peel and finely chop the onion and garlic and place in a small bowl. Add ¼ teaspoons *each* salt and white pepper, mix well and sprinkle over the spinach. Dot with the remaining butter. Fold up the foil to make packets.

Step 2

4 Cook packets on the grill for 8–10 minutes. Sauté the bacon in a skillet until crisp. Drain on paper towels.

5 Remove the fish from the packets and place each fillet on a plate. Place a spinach packet and bacon strips next to each fillet. Garnish with the lemon slices.

Step 3

Preparation: 30 minutes
Grilling: 10 minutes
Per serving: 356 cal; 38 g pro; 17 g fat; 11 g carb.

TYPICALLY GERMAN
Since Northern Germany is bordered by water, seafood plays a main role in the cuisine of the region. The abundant harvest keeps resident chefs and home cooks well supplied with the freshest fruits of the sea.

$\mathscr{B}$ACON-WRAPPED BRATWURST

Called "pølser" in Danish, these hot grilled sausages—here adorned with crispy fried bacon, mustard, and fresh rolls—make everybody's mouth water.

INGREDIENTS
(Serves 4)

- 4 fresh beets
- 4 tablespoons butter, softened
- 1 tablespoon chopped fresh basil
- 1 teaspoon caraway seeds
- ½ teaspoon dried thyme
- salt and pepper
- 8 bratwursts
- 16 bacon strips

IN ADDITION

- sweet and spicy mustards
- fresh rolls

INGREDIENT TIP

If you can find sweet Danish ham, cut it into bite-size pieces and grill it on skewers along with the sausages.

1 Scrub the beets under running cold water, but be careful not to damage the skin (see Cooking Tip). Cook, covered, in a medium saucepan of boiling salted water for 30–40 minutes, depending on their size, until half-done. Drain.

2 Prepare the grill. In a small bowl, combine the butter, basil, caraway seeds, thyme, and ¼ teaspoon each salt and pepper and mix well. Spread 4 sheets of aluminum foil with the herb butter and place a beet on each one. Wrap the foil around the beets securely and grill for 30–40 minutes, until tender.

3 Meanwhile, make diagonal slices into the bratwursts, wrap the bacon around them like garlands. After the beets have grilled for 25–30 minutes, place the bratwursts next to them and grill for 5–10 minutes, turning frequently, until crispy brown.

4 Serve the grilled sausages along with the beets, accompanied by sweet and spicy mustards and fresh rolls.

Step 1

Step 2

Step 3

Preparation: 50 minutes
Grilling: 40 minutes
Per serving: 969 cal; 41 g pro; 83 g fat; 13 g carb.

TYPICALLY DANISH
Meat production is a mainstay of the Danish economy, and their cured meats and sausages are world-famous. Bacon and salami, in particular, are leading exports of Denmark.

COOKING TIP

To prevent the beets from "bleeding," take care not to break the skin while preparing them. This keeps the beets nice and juicy. Just as with baked potatoes, you can press the beets to see if they're ready.

SERVING TIPS

Offer a celery salad with this dish, then finish with a plate of cheeses, such as Esrom and Havarti.

 Enjoy a traditional Danish beer or a shot of ice-cold aquavit.

GRILLED SALMON STEAKS

NORWAY

This mouthwatering fish delicacy—preferably made with wild Atlantic salmon—is the high point of a Norwegian barbecue. A luscious white wine sauce cloaks the tender fish.

INGREDIENTS
(Serves 4)

- 1 tablespoon butter
- 1 tablespoon chopped fresh tarragon
- 4 salmon steaks (about 6-8 ounces *each*)
- 2 tablespoons dry white wine
- 2 tablespoons lemon juice
- white pepper

FOR THE SAUCE
- 1½ sticks (12 tablespoons) butter
- 2 egg yolks
- 3 tablespoons dry white wine
- 1 tablespoon tomato paste
- ½ teaspoon Worcestershire sauce
- salt and white pepper

INGREDIENT TIP
Try the butter sauce without the tomato paste but with finely chopped dill or parsley.

1 Prepare the grill. Place 1 tablespoon butter and the tarragon into a small bowl and mix well. Grease 4 sheets of aluminum foil with the mixture. Brush the salmon steaks with 2 tablespoons wine and the lemon juice; place 1 salmon steak on each sheet of foil. Rub ¼ teaspoon white pepper into each steak. Seal the foil around the fish.

2 Place the salmon packets on the grill and cook for 12–15 minutes. Meanwhile, melt 1½ sticks butter in a small saucepan over low heat. Carefully pour the clear yellow liquid into a bowl; discard the milky portion.

3 Place the egg yolks and 3 tablespoons wine in a heat-proof bowl. Set the bowl over a saucepan of simmering water and beat with a portable electric mixer or a whisk until thick.

4 Remove the bowl from the heat and beat in the clarified butter a little at a time. Beat in the tomato paste, Worcestershire sauce, and ¼ teaspoon *each* salt and white pepper. Serve with the salmon.

Step 1

Step 1

Step 4

Preparation: 40 minutes
Grilling: 15 minutes
Per serving: 743 cal; 42 g pro;
62 g fat; 2 g carb.

TYPICALLY NORWEGIAN
Norwegians heartily enjoy the local harvest from both river and sea. A dinnertime favorite is salmon, which is available in many wonderful variations—cured (gravlax), smoked, blended into a fish mousse, or simply seared on the grill.

COOKING TIP

• Fish is delicate and should be handled carefully. If placed directly on the grill, it will stick and easily burn. For this reason, heavy-duty foil is used.

SERVING TIPS

Steamed carrots and broccoli in a marinade of vinegar and oil are delicious served cold alongside the salmon.

Schnapps is a very popular beverage in Norway and can be served as an accompaniment to fish.

KITCHEN GLOSSARY

Here's everything you need to know for successful grilling, from ingredients and techniques to equipment and tips.

AÏOLI

A rich and flavorful garlicky mayonnaise from the Provence region of southern France. It's often served with fish, meat, and vegetables from the grill.

CONDIMENTS

They're essential for a barbecue, especially if you don't have time to prepare your own sauces. You can find varieties ranging from mild to extremely spicy.

CORNSTARCH

This dense, fine white powder is made from the starch in corn kernels. It's used primarily to thicken sauces as well as in some baked goods.

FISH AND SEAFOOD

Fish is most often grilled as a steak or wrapped whole in aluminum foil. Firm fish, like tuna, can be grilled without foil. Cod and flounder fall apart easily and, along with shrimp, should be cooked in aluminum foil or in a broiling pan or grill basket. Shrimp are also excellent grilled on skewers that are set over foil or in a broiling pan.

HERB BUTTER

Butter mixed with a fresh herb can dress up any grilled meat or fish, and you can spread it on bread or stir it into vegetables. To make your own, stir the herb of your choice, a bit of salt, and garlic, if desired, into soft butter. Refrigerate or freeze until ready to serve.

MARINADE

This magic ingredient for grilling is a seasoned liquid—often containing vinegar, wine, or lemon, and sometimes oil—in which meat steeps. The marinade usually serves to enhance flavor and tenderize meat, though lemon juice tends to make fish firmer. Before they are placed on the grill rack, ingredients should be gently removed from the marinade, which is then usually brushed back on during grilling.

A SUCCESSFUL BARBECUE

The better prepared you are for grilling either outdoors or in, the more time you'll have to spend with your guests.

Decoration
Party lights, banners, garlands, and torches can create a warm, festive atmosphere. Scented candles that drive away mosquitoes can be both practical and attractive.

Drinks
Stock up on chilled beverages—soft drinks, beer, and juice are real winners at an outdoor party. If you don't have a lot of room in your refrigerator, put the drinks in a bathtub filled with water and ice cubes. Don't forget the bottle opener and corkscrew.

For the table
Make sure you have plenty of glasses, silverware, napkins, and plates. You can roll the silverware into the napkins and set them decoratively in a glass. Have serving bowls and implements on hand for salads and desserts.

MEATS FOR GRILLING

Use cuts of meat that will cook quickly—steaks, pork chops, fillets, and ribs all work well on the grill. Other suitable cuts include rump steak and beef or pork tenderloin.

GRILL UTENSILS

Stock up with the proper equipment, and you'll be all set for your next barbecue party.

Aluminum foil

Grilled foods—especially the delicate ingredients—are often wrapped in aluminum foil. Potatoes need to be wrapped so the skins don't burn. It's also a good idea to cover the whole grill with foil. This lets the food cook gently and prevents drippings from falling into the fire.

Charcoal

Charcoal is produced by heating wood in the absence of air. It is designed for a slow, even burn.

Charcoal chimney

In this timesaving device, coals are stacked into a pyramid shape, in which they become intensely hot very quickly after they've been lit. When they're ready, the coals are gently spilled into the grill.

Grill utensils

The basic tools needed for grilling are tongs and a grill handle. Also handy is a cutting board for prepping the ingredients, as well as a marinade bowl and brush, which are kept next to the grill.

Lighting materials

It will take about 30 minutes for the fire to reach the proper temperature for cooking. Lighter fluid is particularly helpful to get the grill started. Don't use gasoline or alcohol to start the fire—the high flames can be very dangerous.

Skewers

These long, thin, pointed rods—which are available in metal or wood as well as in a variety of lengths and sizes—are threaded with pieces of meat, fish, or vegetables for cooking on the grill. Look for skewers that are square or flat rather than round, since they will hold the food more securely when they are moved.

Special matches

You'll be best off using special barbecue matches or chimney matches, since these are particularly long.

Types of grills

There are many varieties to choose from, including the hibachi, gas grill, kettle-shaped charcoal grill, and oven-broiler. Make your choice based on needs of space, your pocketbook, and personal preference. The most important thing is safety. Look for a grill that has been tested to meet the proper safety standards.

Wood coals

Varieties of hardwoods, such as mesquite and applewood, have become quite popular. They can enhance the taste of grilled foods. Some cooks like to mix hardwoods with charcoal to add a nuance of flavor.

TANDOORI

The name given to dishes that are cooked in a tandoor oven, which is made of brick and clay and used throughout the country of India.

TEMPERATURES

The heat of a grill can reach up to 400°F. You can regulate the cooking temperature by adjusting the level of the grill rack.

VEGETABLES

Tomatoes, potatoes, corn, zucchini, and many other vegetables are great barbecue fare. Potatoes should always be grilled in foil, and sweet corn shouldn't be cooked too long or it may lose its flavor.

WORCESTERSHIRE SAUCE

Developed by the English from Indian flavorings, this piquant sauce contains vinegar, molasses, and tamarind among other ingredients.

MENU SUGGESTIONS

Surprise your guests with a full barbecue menu. Our suggestions for appetizers, side dishes, and desserts help you to prepare combinations appropriate to a barbecue from each country.

USA

PEPPER STEAK AND HERBED TOMATOES P. 6
Classic Waldorf Salad
Mixed Berry Pie
— ◆ —

BARBECUED SPARERIBS P. 8
Corn on the Cob
Chocolate Whisky Soufflé
— ◆ —

SCRUMPTIOUS SIDE DISHES P. 10
Grilled Burgers and Chicken
Sweet Potato Pie with Whipped Cream
— ◆ —

AUSTRALIA

FETA-STUFFED CHICKEN BREASTS P. 12
Grilled Eggplant
Cherry Pavlova
— ◆ —

NEW ZEALAND

GARLICKY LAMB CHOPS P. 14
Goat Cheese on French Bread
Luscious Kiwi-Strawberry Salad
— ◆ —

CARIBBEAN

SWORDFISH WITH SPICY SALSA P. 18
Caribbean Avocado Salad
Coco-Lime Sundaes
— ◆ —

MEXICO

STEAK MEXICANA P. 20
Roasted Chiles and Corn
Caramel Flan
— ◆ —

KOREA

SESAME BEEF KABOBS P. 22
Cold Cucumber Soup
Creamy Rice Pudding
— ◆ —

JAPAN

TURKEY AND ASPARAGUS SKEWERS P. 24
Vegetable-Shrimp Tempura
Fresh Fruit
— ◆ —

TOKYO-STYLE STEAK P. 26
Tangy Ginger-Noodle Salad
Green Tea Ice Cream
— ◆ —

INDIA

TANDOORI CHICKEN SKEWERS P. 28
Vegetable-Filled Chapati
Fragrant Mango Delight
— ◆ —

JORDAN

SAVORY MEATBALL KABOBS P. 30
Fava Beans with Tomatoes
Baklava
— ◆ —

LEBANON

GRILLED LEMONY CHICKEN P. 32
Tabbouleh
Orange Ice Dream
— ◆ —

TURKEY

FRAGRANT LAMB KABOBS P. 34
Stuffed Grape Leaves
Watermelon with Honey Cream
— ◆ —

GREECE

LEMON-ROSEMARY CHICKEN P. 36
Greek Country Salad
Brandy-Marinated Figs
— ◆ —

PORTUGAL

TUNA STEAK WITH CAPER SAUCE P. 38
Smoked Ham with Toasts
Honey Almond Tart
— ◆ —

SPAIN

CRISPY CHICKEN WITH RED SAUCE P. 40
Garlic Shrimp with Almond Dip
Citrus Fruit Salad
— ◆ —

FRANCE

PROVENÇAL GRILLED VEGETABLES P. 42
Chicken à la Provençale
Pears Belle Hélène

NUT-CRUSTED LAMB CHOPS P. 44
Broccoli Salad with Roquefort Dressing
Strawberry Swirl
— ◆ —

ITALY

SHRIMP AND GARLIC SKEWERS P. 46
Marinated Mushroom Salad
Tempting Tiramisu
— ◆ —

HERBED PORK CHOPS P. 48
Garlic Bread with Tomato and Basil
Ice Cream Bombe
— ◆ —

GERMANY

PEPPERY STEAK AND CHEESY ZUCCHINI P. 52
Pretzels with Horseradish Dip
Summer Fruit Salad
— ◆ —

TENDER COD IN FOIL P. 54
Potato Salad with Cucumbers
Rhubarb Strawberry Treat

DENMARK

BACON-WRAPPED BRATWURST P. 56
Shrimp Salad
Summer Fruit Cheesecake

NORWAY

GRILLED SALMON STEAKS P. 58
Cucumber Dill Salad
Red Currant Cake
— ◆ —

ECIPE INDEX

Photo Credits

Book cover and recipe photos:
©International Masters Publishers AB
Eising Food Photography, Dorothee Gôdert, Ulrich Kerth, Manuel Schnell.
Agency photographs:
Introduction: Kerth, page 5 bottom left.
Look: Dressler, page 5 upper middle.
Mauritius: Rossenbach, page 5 middle left.
Superphoto: Lucas, pages 4, 5 above.
Tony Stone: Schert, page 4 middle left.
Transglobe: Weber, page 4 lower middle.
Photos for the "Typically" sections:
Bavaria: Ball, page 34.
Bilderberg: Aurora, page 8; Baumgartel, page 25; Bossemeyer, page 46.

ISBN 1-886614-86-5